OXFORD
Children's History of the World

THE
20TH
CENTURY
WORLD

Neil Grant

OXFORD
UNIVERSITY PRESS

OXFORD
UNIVERSITY PRESS

Great Clarendon Street, Oxford OX2 6DP

Oxford University Press is a department of the University of Oxford.
It furthers the University's objective of excellence in research, scholarship,
and education by publishing worldwide in

Oxford New York

Athens Auckland Bangkok Bogotá Buenos Aires Kolkata
Cape Town Chennai Dar es Salaam Delhi Florence Hong Kong Istanbul
Karachi Kuala Lumpur Madrid Melbourne Mexico City Mumbai
Nairobi Paris São Paulo Shanghai Singapore Taipei Tokyo Toronto Warsaw

with associated companies in Berlin Ibadan

Oxford is a registered trade mark of Oxford University Press
in the UK and in certain other countries

First published 2001
Some material in this book was previously
published in Children's History of the World 2000

British Library Cataloguing in Publication Data available

Paperback ISBN 0-19-910826-9

1 3 5 7 9 10 8 6 4 2

Printed in Malaysia

CONSULTANTS
Mike Corbishley
Dr. Narayani Gupta
Dr. Rick Halpern
Dr. Douglas H. Johnson
Rosemary Kelly
James Mason

Contents

How to use this book

This book is divided into double-page spreads, each on a different subject. At the end of the book there is a Timeline. This shows at a glance the developments in different regions of the world during the period covered by the section. There is also a Who's Who page, which gives short biographies of the most important people of the period, a Glossary of important words, and an Index.

Dates here show the time in history when the events took place.

The title describes the subject of the spread, like a newspaper headline.

The first paragraph sets the scene, explaining what the spread is about and why it is important.

Photographs and illustrations show paintings, objects, places, people and scenes from the past.

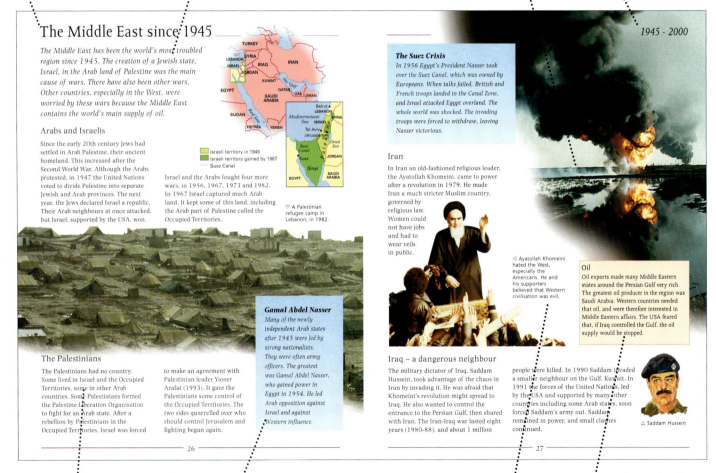

The Middle East since 1945

The Middle East has been the world's most troubled region since 1945. The creation of a Jewish state, Israel, in the Arab land of Palestine was the main cause of wars. There have also been other wars. Other countries, especially in the West, were worried by these wars because the Middle East contains the world's main supply of oil.

Arabs and Israelis

Since the early 20th century Jews had settled in Arab Palestine, their ancient homeland. This increased after the Second World War. Although the Arabs protested, in 1947 the United Nations voted to divide Palestine into separate Jewish and Arab provinces. The next year, the Jews declared Israel a republic. Their Arab neighbours at once attacked, but Israel, supported by the USA, won.

■ Israeli territory in 1949
■ Israeli territory gained by 1967
— Suez Canal

Israel and the Arabs fought four more wars, in 1956, 1967, 1973 and 1982. In 1967 Israel captured much Arab land. It kept some of this land, including the Arab part of Palestine called the Occupied Territories.

▽ A Palestinian refugee camp in Lebanon, in 1982.

The Palestinians

The Palestinians had no country. Some lived in Israel and the Occupied Territories, some in other Arab countries. Some Palestinians formed the Palestine Liberation Organisation to fight for an Arab state. After a rebellion by Palestinians in the Occupied Territories, Israel was forced to make an agreement with Palestinian leader Yasser Arafat (1993). It gave the Palestinians some control of the Occupied Territories. The two sides quarrelled over who should control Jerusalem and fighting began again.

Gamal Abdel Nasser
Many of the newly independent Arab states after 1945 were led by strong nationalists. They were often army officers. The greatest was Gamal Abdel Nasser, who gained power in Egypt in 1954. He led Arab opposition against Israel and against Western influence.

The Suez Crisis
In 1956 Egypt's President Nasser took over the Suez Canal, which was owned by Europeans. When talks failed, British and French troops landed in the Canal Zone, and Israel attacked Egypt overland. The whole world was shocked. The invading troops were forced to withdraw, leaving Nasser victorious.

Iran

In Iran an old-fashioned religious leader, the Ayatollah Khomeini, came to power after a revolution in 1979. He made Iran a much stricter Muslim country, governed by religious law. Women could not have jobs and had to wear veils in public.

◁ Ayatollah Khomeini hated the West, especially the Americans. He and his supporters believed that Western civilisation was evil.

Oil
Oil exports made many Middle Eastern states around the Persian Gulf very rich. The greatest oil producer in the region was Saudi Arabia. Western countries needed that oil, and were therefore interested in Middle Eastern affairs. The USA feared that, if Iraq controlled the Gulf, the oil supply would be stopped.

Iraq – a dangerous neighbour

The military dictator of Iraq, Saddam Hussein, took advantage of the chaos in Iran by invading it. He was afraid that Khomeini's revolution might spread to Iraq. He also wanted to control the entrance to the Persian Gulf, then shared with Iran. The Iran-Iraq war lasted eight years (1980-88), and about 1 million people were killed. In 1990 Saddam invaded a smaller neighbour on the Gulf, Kuwait. In 1991 the forces of the United Nations, led by the USA and supported by many other countries including some Arab states, soon forced Saddam's army out. Saddam remained in power, and small clashes continued.

△ Saddam Hussein

1945 - 2000

26

27

The text is divided into short blocks, each with its own heading. They describe one part of the main subject of the spread.

Coloured boxes give more details about major events or important people linked to the subject.

Captions describe the illustrations and how they relate to the main text.

Fact boxes list key events associated with the subject.

Many pages also have a map, to show the country or region where the events took place.

Introduction

Over the past 100 years, the speed at which the world has changed has steadily increased. If people who were alive in 1900 could return today, they would be amazed. Today, American and Russian scientists are building a huge space station in orbit around the Earth. In 1900 the aeroplane had not been invented, hardly anyone owned a motor car, there was no television, no radio, no cinema; nuclear power and computers were far in the future. The huge advances made by science and medicine in 20th century meant that people lived longer. They were richer, with more money for holidays and entertainment. Life was more comfortable.

Not everyone had an easier time. Life did not change much for a farming family in a poor country. In 2000 children were still dying not because they had few doctors or hospitals, but because they had no clean water to drink. The gap between rich and poor was still huge.

Some progress was made towards greater fairness. The position of women improved. In 1900 women took no part in government (they could not even vote), or in business or skilled jobs. A woman doctor or lawyer was almost unheard-of. By 2000 most of these disadvantages had disappeared, especially in industrialised countries, but also in others, including Islamic countries.

In 1900 many countries, including nearly all of Africa, were ruled by Europeans. Racial prejudice was common. One hundred years after slavery ended, black people in America were still 'second-class citizens'. That began to change after the civil-rights movement in the 1960s. At the same time, European colonies became independent. Although racial prejudice had not disappeared, it was no longer supported by laws and governments.

Changes are not always improvements. Medicine improved enormously, but in the 1990s millions died of a disease called AIDS, which was unknown in 1900. Progress in technology brought many good things, but it also damaged the natural environment, which was threatened by human activities.

Technology also provided new weapons. More people died in wars than in any earlier century. Rulers such as Stalin and Hitler caused the deaths of millions of their own subjects. But Hitler's Nazis were defeated in the Second World War, and Stalinist communism collapsed in 1989. By 2000, the states of the world had achieved greater co-operation through organisations such as the United Nations or the European Union. Although smaller wars were common, world war seemed unlikely.

The World in 1900

By 1900 the rich countries of the West controlled world affairs. It was a time of peace, but the world was less safe than it seemed. World business went through sharp ups and downs, and in Europe the rival powers formed two hostile groups.

The state of the World

The biggest change since 1800 was the rise of industry, which had made the Western nations rich and powerful. People could travel almost anywhere in the world in a much shorter time, and radio would soon make it possible to pass messages around the world in a few minutes. Yet for poorer people, even those ruled by European states, life had hardly changed at all. In Europe itself, nations remained as divided as ever, and their conflicts would soon plunge the world into war.

The Mexican Revolution

In 1910, the Mexican dictator Porfirio Diaz was driven out after 30 years in power. The Revolution lasted ten years. The biggest quarrel was over land. It was nearly all owned by a few landowners, but others wanted a share. Leaders rose and fell. They included landowners and generals as well as Pancho Villa, who led the cowboys. Emiliano Zapata led the peasants, who farmed the land but owned none of it. From 1920, Mexico was united under a new form of government.

▽ In 1900, to the well-off people visiting the World Exhibition in Paris, the world seemed peaceful and prosperous. They looked forward to a life of peace and comfort. But the 20th century had unpleasant shocks in store.

△ International sport became possible when rules for games such as football (soccer) were agreed. Unlike team games, the athletics events at the first modern Olympic Games in 1896 were much the same as in ancient Greece. This picture is from the 1912 Games.

The power of money

Europe's domination of the world economy rested on the power and wealth of Great Britain. The British navy controlled the seas and guarded shipping routes. London was the world centre of banking and business. The railways of South America were built with British money (and often by British engineers). France, Britain and other rich European states often financed industrial development in other countries, including the USA. French companies financed much of Russia's industrial development.

Only a few people – mainly the middle classes in Western countries – enjoyed the benefits of Europe's economic success. A peasant who became a factory worker was more likely to become unemployed in the 'booms' and 'slumps' that made some firms rich and others bankrupt. Most 19th-century governments believed that they should not interfere in business. Free competition between firms was supposed to keep prices down. This did not always work, especially as companies got together to form business 'empires'.

The confident West

Europeans' success in creating wealth and power made them believe they were superior to non-Europeans. Their way of life seemed far in advance of other continents. Some people believed that education could pass these advantages on to other nations. Others believed that European civilisation was heading for a breakdown.

▽ Nearly every European country had free primary schools for all children by 1914.

Tension in Europe

By 1900 Germany had overtaken Great Britain as Europe's largest industrial power. Its neighbours, France and Russia, feared the new German Empire and formed an alliance, which Britain joined later. Germany, in turn, felt threatened by that alliance but had its own partners in Austria and Italy. Besides having a well-equipped army, Germany began building a navy to challenge the British, and wanted more colonies in Africa. There were several tense international incidents, when the two rival alliances came close to war.

The most dangerous region was the Balkans – the small countries of south-east Europe which were breaking free from the Ottoman Empire. Serbia and Bulgaria especially were competing against each other for land and power. Austria and Russia both wanted influence in the region too. Two Balkan wars in 1912-13 ended with Serbia as the most powerful Balkan state. This situation alarmed Austria because, by ethnic background and religion, the Serbs were linked to Russia.

The First World War

The First World War was the first general war in Europe for 100 years. It was fought with the new weapons and explosives of modern industry, by armies made up of every young man fit enough to fight. More than 8 million soldiers were killed.

Allied Powers
Central Powers
neutral country
—— Western Front in 1918
—— Eastern Front in 1918

△ Europe during the First World War. Countries had formed alliances for defence, as a safety measure. A small incident set off war between them.

Murder in Sarajevo

In June 1914 the heir to the Austrian throne was assassinated in Sarajevo, Bosnia, by a Serb terrorist. The Austrians blamed the Serbian government and declared war. Russia came to the support of Serbia, Germany supported Austria and also attacked France, Russia's ally. Britain, with its empire, came to the support of France.

A world war

Other countries were drawn in. Italy joined the Allies (Britain and France) and fought the Austrians in southern Europe. Russia stopped fighting after its revolution in 1917, but the USA joined the Allies. So did Australia, New Zealand and Japan, while Turkey joined Germany and Austria. Although the heaviest fighting was in Europe, there was some fighting against the Turks. The Arabs, with British support, rebelled against their Turkish rulers in the Middle East.

German submarines attacked ships of other nations, including harmless passenger ships. This brought the USA into the war. There was only one great naval battle between the mighty British and German fleets, at Jutland (1916). By 1918, the European nations were worn out. German civilians were starving, and there were mutinies in the French army. In November, revolution broke out in Germany and at the same time, the fleet mutinied. Germany surrendered.

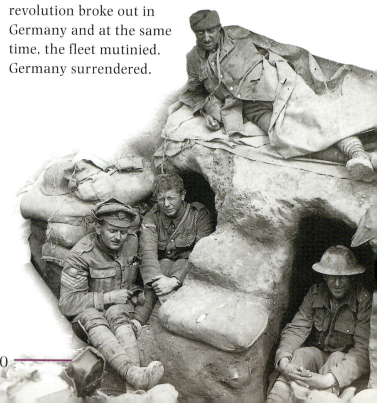

The trenches

At first, people thought the war would be short. Instead, the fighting became bogged down. The soldiers faced each other from defensive trenches. The killing power of machine guns and explosive shells made attack almost impossible, and generals could not break out of this pattern. They tried poison gas, but it could only be used when the wind was in the right direction. Later in the war, they tried tanks.

The home front

Earlier wars had been mostly fought by professional armies, while life at home continued much as usual. But the First World War involved civilians as well as soldiers. Because nearly all young men were called up to fight, women took on their jobs – especially in the factories making weapons, on farms and in transport. They proved just as good as men, sometimes better. They seldom complained or got drunk. The cause of women's rights took a giant leap forward.

◁ Women doing skilled work in an aircraft factory in 1917. This was the first war in which aircraft played an important part.

Winners and losers

Over 15 million people died in the war. Germany was in chaos. France was not much better. The Allies were deep in debt, mainly to the USA. The Versailles peace treaty (1919) created new states such as Czechoslovakia and Yugoslavia, and set up the League of Nations to settle international quarrels. The League placed provinces of the defeated Turkish Empire under French or British rule, with a promise of future independence. The peacemakers blamed Germany for the war, and ordered the new German republic to pay huge sums for the damage caused. That made it hard for Germany to recover. The biggest 'winner' was the USA, where war caused rapid industrial growth. By 1919 the USA was clearly the most powerful nation in the world.

△ Early tanks often broke down, and not many had been built. But military planners saw that they might be the answer to the horrible stalemate of trench warfare.

◁ Apart from rats, mud, shells and poison gas, soldiers were protected if they stayed in their trenches. But when they went 'over the top' to make an attack, they were easily killed. In 1915 about 2 million British and French soldiers were killed in the battles of the Somme. The biggest advance made in any attack was only three miles.

The Irish Rebellion

At Easter 1916, Irish republicans rebelled against British rule. The British quickly crushed the Easter Rising, but afterwards, nationalist feelings in Ireland grew stronger. The republican party, Sinn Fein, won many seats in elections and formed an underground government. In 1921, after three years of violence, Britain agreed to a separate government for Ireland, except for six, mainly Protestant counties in the north, which refused to join the Catholic Irish Free State.

The Russian Revolution

In 1917 the people of Russia rebelled against their ruler, the tsar, in a revolution. The result was a completely new system of government, called communism. It was supposed to give power to ordinary working people, but instead just a few men controlled the country by fear.

The coming of revolution

In 1900 Russia was a backward country compared with western Europe. It was something like France before the French Revolution. The peasants were no longer serfs, but their life was still poor and primitive. They had no say in the government. The government was neither efficient nor honest. The tsar, who was supposed to be all-powerful, seemed weak. In the cities, strikes and riots were frequent. Educated people believed that big reforms were necessary in Russia.

In 1905, Russia's shameful defeat in a war with Japan provoked rebellion. The tsar promised to set up a more democratic government, but this did not happen. In 1917, with Russians suffering in the First World War, rebellion broke out again. This time the tsar was deposed and a republic was declared. Six months later, in a second revolution, the Bolsheviks took over the government. Russia was renamed the Union of Soviet Socialist Republics (the USSR), often referred to as the Soviet Union.

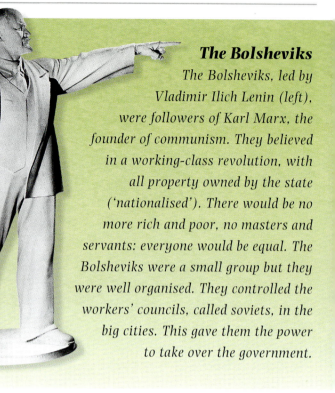

The Bolsheviks

The Bolsheviks, led by Vladimir Ilich Lenin (left), were followers of Karl Marx, the founder of communism. They believed in a working-class revolution, with all property owned by the state ('nationalised'). There would be no more rich and poor, no masters and servants: everyone would be equal. The Bolsheviks were a small group but they were well organised. They controlled the workers' councils, called soviets, in the big cities. This gave them the power to take over the government.

▷ November 1917: Bolshevik 'Red Guards' stormed the Winter Palace in St Petersburg. The government surrendered, but the fighting came later.

Civil war

After the Revolution, the Bolsheviks made peace with Germany. But there was no peace inside the Soviet Union. Anti-Bolshevik forces, with help from abroad, fought for three years against the 'Red Army' organised by Lenin's associate, Trotsky.

The Bolsheviks expected communist revolutions to break out all over Europe but, except for a small one in Germany, they did not. However, communist parties did exist in other countries. As allies of the Soviet government, they worked for an international revolution.

▷ A defendant (left) stands before the prosecutors at a state trial in 1931. Innocent people confessed to 'crimes against the state' in order to save their families from punishment.

Russia under Stalin

After the death of Lenin, Joseph Stalin, as secretary of the Communist Party, increased the power of the Party and banned all other parties. By 1930 he was more powerful than the tsar had been. He built up a huge, efficient secret police, and his rule was based on fear. He treated all his opponents as traitors. He ordered millions of people to be killed, or sent to prison camps in Siberia.

Stalin reorganised the USSR as a communist country. In agriculture, independent farms were forced into large 'collectives' run very badly by Party officials. Millions died of starvation. Stalin was determined to make the USSR a great industrial power that could challenge the USA. Industry did increase but, as in farming, the state grew more powerful while the workers were no better off. Under Stalin, only Party officials lived well.

△ The government used art for propaganda for the workers' state. This May Day poster shows workers marching over symbols for wealth, and the tsar and his government.

Between the World Wars

The war caused more problems than it solved. After 1918, Europe was a more dangerous place than before. Democratic governments failed to solve people's problems. Some people turned to communism, represented by Soviet Russia, and others to an extreme form of nationalism.

The 1920s

Living standards rose in the West in the 1920s, the age of jazz, nightclubs and cinema. The American 'Model T' Ford was the first mass-produced car, which ordinary families could afford. More women went out to work. Few of them were lawyers or doctors, but many were wage-earners. Before 1914, working women were mostly servants. Their new jobs brought greater independence as well as higher pay. Although there were fewer servants, machines such as vacuum cleaners and gas or electric cookers made household tasks easier.

△ In the 1920s people wanted to forget the war. They set out to have a good time. Women especially felt a new sense of freedom. The war had made them more independent.

▽ The Great Depression ended the fun. Respectable Americans lost their jobs, their savings and their property. They had to live in shanty towns like this one in Seattle, Washington.

The Great Depression

The capitalist system always had booms and slumps. The worst slump ever began in 1929, with a sharp fall in the value of shares on the New York stock market. The effects spread quickly. Banks and businesses collapsed. People who had been rich suddenly had nothing. The Great Depression affected non-industrial countries too, as the market for their exports almost disappeared. Communists believed that the whole capitalist system was collapsing, as Marx had said it would. But by the mid-1930s, business was beginning to recover.

△ The Fascist leader Mussolini thought of himself as a kind of modern Roman emperor. Fascists believed in power and the glory of the nation. They cared little for ordinary human rights.

Fascism

In countries such as Italy and Germany, the war and the terms of the peace treaty (1919) caused grave problems. Democratic governments seemed unable to solve them, and many people were attracted to extreme nationalist parties. In Italy the Fascist party led by Mussolini gained power in 1922, after a threatening march on Rome. Mussolini ended democracy and made himself a dictator. He promised to make Italy a great power, and set out to create an empire in Africa, conquering Ethiopia.

The Nazis

Adolf Hitler was the head of the National Socialists (Nazis) in Germany. Like Mussolini, he won votes because he promised to solve the country's terrible problems. Then he abolished parliament and made himself a dictator, supported by brutal secret police. The Nazis crushed, or even murdered, all who opposed them, including many communists. They were also racists of an extreme kind. They hated Jews, gypsies, Slavs and all others who they said belonged to an 'inferior race'. Hitler aimed to create a new German empire. He set out to make the country powerful, by building up the army, navy and air force, although that was forbidden by the peace treaty of 1919.

Fascism in the Far East

Other countries, such as Spain and Argentina, came under some form of fascist rule in the 1930s. In Japan, many army officers held fascist ideas, and many ordinary Japanese believed that their economic problems could only be solved by force. The government was weak, and violence was growing. Three prime ministers were murdered between 1918 and 1932. Military men gained influence in government. In 1931 the army took over Chinese Manchuria, and further aggression led to war with China. Japan also made agreements with fascist Germany and Italy. When war broke out in Europe in 1939, Japan seized the chance to invade French and British colonies in south-east Asia.

The Spanish Civil War

Spain became a republic in 1931, but the country was badly split between different groups. The government made some reforms, then cancelled them. There were protests, riots and revolts. The government was losing control, and an army rebellion set off three years of civil war (1936-39). Socialists, communists and other left-wing groups supported the government. The Church, landowners and the army supported the rebels, who also received aid from Hitler and Mussolini. General Franco's victory began a fascist dictatorship which lasted until his death in 1975.

The Arts and Entertainment

From the late 19th century great changes took place in the arts, music and literature, mainly in the West. At the same time, new forms of entertainment were invented for ordinary people, who were now better educated, better paid and had more time for hobbies and amusements.

△ Pablo Picasso (1881-1973), the most famous painter of the 20th century. Some people said his art was ugly and unrealistic. But artists were not trying to paint realistic pictures.

◁ In cities around the world, huge buildings in new styles and materials appeared among older, more decorative ones. This is in Kuala Lumpur, Malaysia.

Painting and sculpture

Around 1900 many groups of artists broke away from the European style of art, which had not changed much since the Renaissance. If you wanted a picture of something, you could take a photograph! So artists experimented with new ways of seeing. One development was abstract art, which contained shapes and colours but nothing that can be seen in nature.

Architecture

From the 1920s 'modern' architects, like other artists, wanted to break away from the old styles of building. They believed that a building should not be decorative, but should look like what it was, even if it were a slaughter-house. They were able to use new kinds of material, such as concrete, glass and steel, and new engineering techniques. They designed some interesting buildings, quite different from any earlier style. Many cheaper buildings which were influenced by the modern style were not successful, especially those built after the Second World War. By the 1990s, the best new buildings were less severe in appearance.

Literature and books

The wish to experiment affected all the arts. Experimental novelists stopped telling stories and tried to get inside the mind and feelings of their characters. Others experimented with language itself. A famous example is James Joyce's *Finnegan's Wake* (1939).

At the same time, better education and more spare time created millions of new readers who wanted simpler stories. This demand resulted in new types of popular novels, such as detective stories and science fiction. In spite of other forms of entertainment, more and more books of all sorts were published during the 20th century.

Music

In music, American jazz became very popular in the 1920s, along with dance music. In the West, young people, like their parents, had more money. That opened new opportunities for business, especially in the entertainment industry. It was helped by advances in sound recording – long-playing records (1948), stereo sound, magnetic-tape cassettes and compact discs (1983). These advances gave rise to trends such as pop music, which appealed directly to the young but was often disliked by older people. Pop music grew into an industry from the 1950s, thanks to advances in sound recording and (later) video, and to more money in teenagers' pockets. After the Beatles leading pop stars, like top sports people and fashion designers, were as rich and famous as the great Hollywood film stars.

△ The Beatles were four boys from Liverpool, England, who became the most successful pop group of the 1960s. Young people bought their records in millions.

Broadcasting

Radio broadcasting spread across the world in the 1920s, providing entertainment at home. Television was invented in the 1930s but did not get going in most countries until the 1950s, delayed by the Second World War. By 1980 nearly every home had a TV. Further advances in technology provided video recorders, and a wider choice of radio and TV channels, broadcast through cables and by satellite, as well as aerials. A new method, digital broadcasting, offered more TV channels and opened other opportunities by 2000. Homes had many new machines and instruments - for cooking and housework, as well as for entertainment.

Cinema

Moving pictures were invented about 1890. Although films had no sound until 1928, cinema was the chief entertainment for working people between the world wars, along with spectator sports. Hollywood films showed a richer, more glamorous world, and the cinemas themselves were more like palaces. More recently, the Indian film industry, based in Bombay ('Bollywood'), produced more films than any other country.

Germany and the Second World War

Hitler rebuilt a powerful Germany in the 1930s, but his efforts to enlarge the borders of his new German empire led to a new world war, only 20 years after the peace settlement agreed at Versailles in 1919.

◁ German schoolchildren carrying Nazi banners welcome Hitler to the Sudetenland. In September 1938 Britain and France agreed that this part of Czechoslovakia should be given to Germany.

Hitler and Europe

The Versailles treaty after the First World War was meant to stop Germany becoming powerful again. But Hitler took no notice. In 1936 German troops marched into the Rhineland, which was forbidden by the treaty. In 1938, in a peaceful invasion, Hitler took over Austria, also forbidden. He accused Czechoslovakia and Poland of mistreating their German-speaking citizens, and threatened them with war.

No other great power was willing to stop Hitler. The USA wanted nothing to do with European affairs. Soviet Russia was the enemy of both sides and hoped for war between them. Mussolini's Italy was Hitler's ally. That left only the European democracies, Great Britain and France. They had problems of their own, and their greatest desire was to avoid another war. So, while protesting against Hitler's illegal acts, they took no action against him.

Czechoslovakia and Poland

In September 1938 a summit meeting was held in Munich, to try to prevent an attack on Czechoslovakia. Without consulting the Czechs, the British and French leaders agreed that Germany could have the Czech Sudetenland, where most German-speakers lived. The Sudetenland also contained Czechoslovakia's border defences. Six months later Hitler's troops marched into the Czech capital, Prague, and took over the country without a fight. Britain and France now realised that Hitler could not be trusted. They promised to support Poland, which was also threatened. The world was shocked in August 1939 when Nazi Germany signed an agreement with its arch-enemy, Stalin's Soviet Russia. With no danger of a Russian attack, the Germans could then safely invade Poland. But when the Germans did invade Poland in September 1939, Britain and France declared war.

The conquest of Europe

Britain and France could not help the Poles, who were quickly overrun. Events soon showed that they could not stop the German armies anywhere else. Within a year, the Germans had taken Denmark, Norway, Belgium and the Netherlands. In June 1940 France surrendered and German forces occupied most of France. A French government at Vichy governed the south-east and the French colonies, but it took its orders from the Germans. The whole of Europe was then under control of the Axis (the German-Italian alliance) except for Great Britain, and a few neutral countries including Soviet Russia. The British had an inspiring leader, Winston Churchill. They were supported by their overseas empire and protected by the English Channel. The Germans could not invade unless they first controlled the air. In the Battle of Britain (1940), the first big air battle, the German air force failed to win that control.

Blitzkrieg

The Germans invented a new kind of fighting (Blitzkrieg, 'lightning war'), far more effective than trench warfare. Fast-moving columns of tanks, supported by aircraft, drove deep into the enemy's country. Tanks and aircraft had played only a small part in the First World War.

◁ The German conquest of Europe. Apart from neutral states, Germany invaded every European country except the United Kingdom. They also captured much of North Africa.

- ── German boundary in 1939
- ▇ area under German control in 1942
- ▇ area under Allied control in 1942
- ▢ neutral country

◁ German troops marching up the Champs Elysée, the ceremonial avenue of Paris, in 1940. The Germans allowed a French government at Vichy, but it was under German orders.

Invasion of Russia

Hitler's ambition was to win more land in eastern Europe for his German empire. In spite of the German-Soviet agreement of 1939, Hitler saw Soviet Russia, not Britain, as his main enemy. The Russians were not only communists, they were also Slavs – a second-class people according to the Nazis. In 1941 the Germans invaded the Soviet Union. Russia was a much larger country than Germany, but there too the German forces advanced swiftly. They reached St Petersburg and Moscow, before fierce defence and the freezing Russian winter brought them to a stop. Stalin's government was surprised by the invasion and its defences were weak, but the Russians moved many of their arms factories across the Ural Mountains into Siberia, where they would be safe from the Germans.

The Second World War

The Second World War lasted for seven years. From 1941 both the USA and the Soviet Union were fighting with the British Empire. Those two giant countries had so many men and such huge industries that the Allies were bound to win in the end.

▽ To escape German bombs, 1.5 million English children were moved from the most dangerous parts of London and other cities to villages in the countryside.

War at sea

The USA opposed Japanese conquests in Asia in 1937-41. The Japanese expected war with the USA sooner or later, so they launched a surprise attack on the US naval base at Pearl Harbor in Hawaii (December 1941). Germany supported Japan, and the USA entered the war.

Like the German Blitzkrieg in Europe, the USA and Japan fought a new kind of war in the Pacific. Early battles were fought between fleets of aircraft carriers and their warplanes. The Japanese started to retreat after their defeat at the Battle of Midway (1942). In the Atlantic, German submarines and cruisers attacked the Allied merchant fleets bringing supplies from North America to Britain. But US shipyards produced ships three times as fast as the German submarines could sink them.

△ US troops landing in the Pacific. The Japanese fought fiercely to defend every island against the US advance in 1942-45.

War in Europe and North Africa

Until 1942 the Axis powers seemed to be winning the war. Then the tide turned. The Russians trapped a large German army at Stalingrad and forced them to surrender early in 1943. The British had been driven out of Europe in 1940, but fought in North Africa. They defeated a German army at the Battle of Alamein (1942). Next year, the Allies drove the Germans out of North Africa. From there Allied forces invaded Italy and overthrew Mussolini. The Italians surrendered, but German troops occupied Italy and held up the Allied advance.

The main Allied invasion of Europe began in June 1944. It was the biggest invasion in history. Under the command of US General Eisenhower, the Allied forces landed in Normandy and drove the Germans back. They freed France from German rule in August, and invaded Germany. As Allied forces advanced from the west, the Soviet 'Red Army' drove the Germans out of Russia and Poland, and invaded Germany from the east. By April 1945 the Red Army was in Berlin. Hitler shot himself, and the German armies surrendered.

The atom bomb

In 1944-45 US forces continued to advance against the Japanese in the Pacific, while the British reconquered Burma. It was obvious that Japan was losing, but many Japanese soldiers believed that defeat is worse than death, and refused to give up. To prevent thousands of American lives being lost, the US government forced Japan to surrender. They used a frightful new weapon that scientists had recently developed: the atom bomb. Two bombs were dropped, on the cities of Hiroshima and Nagasaki, destroying practically every building and tens of thousands of people in a large area. (Allied bombers had caused greater destruction of German and Japanese cities earlier, but not with a single bomb.)

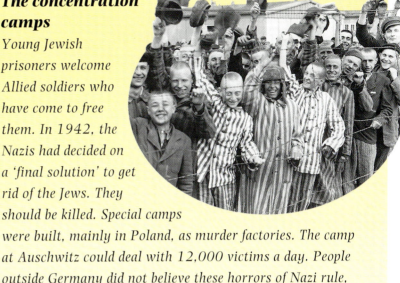

The concentration camps

Young Jewish prisoners welcome Allied soldiers who have come to free them. In 1942, the Nazis had decided on a 'final solution' to get rid of the Jews. They should be killed. Special camps were built, mainly in Poland, as murder factories. The camp at Auschwitz could deal with 12,000 victims a day. People outside Germany did not believe these horrors of Nazi rule, until the Allied and Soviet armies captured the camps in 1945. Altogether, about 6 million Jews died in Nazi Europe.

European failure

The world war destroyed Nazi rule, although it strengthened Stalin's equally murderous regime. From 1945 Stalin controlled the countries of eastern Europe that the Red Army had reconquered from the Germans.

The horrors of the first half of the 20th century made some people think that European civilisation was dying. Certainly, Europeans no longer ruled the world. After the disasters of the two world wars, they could not claim the right to govern other countries. They could not even control their own affairs. By 1945, it was obvious the two victorious 'superpowers', the Soviet Union and the USA, would decide the future of Europe.

◁ In June 1944 hundreds of ships, protected by thousands of aircraft, carried Allied armies from British ports to the beaches of Normandy. It was the beginning of the final campaign, which ended nearly a year later with Germany's surrender.

The End of European Empires

In 1939 European nations ruled nearly all of Africa and much of Asia. By 1970 most of these colonies had become independent states. In some places the change was peaceful. In others it happened only after savage wars.

Self-rule

Most Europeans admitted when establishing their colonies that they would become independent – one day, perhaps far in the future. In 1919 former Turkish provinces such as Syria and Palestine had been placed under French and British rule, but only to prepare them for independence. Britain had also promised independence to India, but progress was slow. After 1945, the old imperial countries came under more pressure to give up their empires. This pressure came not only from the people they ruled, but also from the two great world powers, the Soviet Union and the USA.

India

The Indian National Congress was founded in 1885 and led the struggle for Indian independence. At first it was a tiny party demanding reforms. In the 1920s it gained more support thanks to the leadership of Gandhi, but many Muslims left Congress to form their own nationalist party, the Muslim League. The British made some reforms, giving Indians a bigger part in government, but in 1942 Congress demanded full independence. By 1945 the new British government was eager to leave. But the division between Hindus and Muslims could not be healed. As a result, British India became independent (1947) as two states, Hindu India and Muslim Pakistan. Terrible violence took place between Hindus and Muslims in some areas, with many thousands slaughtered or driven from their homes. The two countries remained on bad terms and fought three short wars between 1947 and 1971. Pakistan itself was divided into two parts. In 1971 India supported East Pakistan when it broke away to become Bangladesh.

△ Gandhi leads a protest march against a British tax, in 1930. He was as much a holy man as a politician, and wanted to change people's hearts – Hindus, Muslims and British alike. His protests were never violent and he dreamed of a country where all races, religions and castes could live together in peace.

Asia

The Japanese had conquered many European colonies in Asia. Although the Europeans returned in 1945, most colonies gained independence within a few years. In 1948 Britain agreed independence for Burma and Sri Lanka (not conquered by Japan). Indonesia had forced out the Dutch by 1949, and the Philippines became independent of the USA in 1946. In South-East Asia things were more difficult, due partly to communist movements. Malaysia became independent in 1963. France withdrew from Cambodia (1949), Laos (1953) and Vietnam (1954), though civil wars continued.

Black Africa

Nearly the whole of Africa was under colonial control until the 1960s. Many colonies remained on friendly terms with their former rulers. But they had special difficulties. Some were very poor, with few resources, low standards of education and not enough people skilled in government. Because the colonial rulers had formed colonies without considering the boundaries between different peoples, the new states contained rival groups who did not easily act together. Governments were unstable, and small groups or military dictators came to hold power. These people made themselves rich but made their country still poorer. Nigeria, the largest, contained different nations and religions. It became a federal republic, but quarrels between the different regions led to civil war and dictatorship.

dates of independence
- before 1940
- 1940–1949
- 1950–1959
- 1960–1969
- 1970–1979
- 1980–1989
- after 1989

△ The countries of modern Africa. In 1940 Egypt and Liberia alone were officially independent, although Ethiopia was a colony only from 1936.

▽ In new states some people grew rich, but most stayed poor. In places such as Lagos, Nigeria, slums grew up next to modern city centres.

White Africans

The cause of independence brought the greatest violence to countries where many whites had settled. In Algeria, nationalists fought a long and savage civil war against the French authorities and the many inhabitants of French descent. The great French war leader and statesman, Charles de Gaulle, returning to power in 1958, saw that the only solution was for France to withdraw. South Africa, an independent republic from 1961, had been a 'white' country since the 16th century. It adopted the policy called apartheid, 'separateness', which placed all power and wealth in the hands of the white minority. Rhodesia, a British colony, was refused independence because the whites refused to share power with the black majority. After a long civil war (1965-79) the colonial government admitted defeat, and Rhodesia became the republic of Zimbabwe.

The United Nations and the Cold War

The United Nations (UN) was founded in 1945 as a place where quarrels between nations could be discussed and war prevented. Its work was made difficult by the enmity of the two 'superpowers', the USA and the Soviet Union, each supported by its allies.

▽ Some of the UN's most important work was done by special departments, or agencies. These included the World Bank, which lends money to poor countries, and UNICEF, which aims to improve education and free communication, as well as protecting people's traditional way of life.

The United Nations

The United Nations replaced the old League of Nations. Nearly every nation became a member of its General Assembly. Decisions were made by the Security Council, dominated by the rival superpowers. As the UN depended on its members for support, it had little real power. It could organise a small force to keep the peace in local quarrels around the world, but it had no permanent army. When it did fight a war, as in the Gulf (1991), the 'UN Forces' were mainly US.

members of NATO and
the Warsaw Pact in 1960

- [green] NATO countries (also including USA, Canada and Iceland)
- [purple] Warsaw Pact countries
- [yellow] neutral countries

▷ When the Hungarian people rebelled against Communist control in 1956, Soviet forces invaded and crushed the rebellion. When Alexander Dubcek introduced a freer form of communism in Czechoslovakia in 1968, Soviet tanks moved in again (right), and Dubcek was removed.

The Berlin airlift

The division of Germany was one cause of conflict. Although Berlin lay inside communist East Germany, the western half of the city, like West Germany, was occupied by the Western allies. In 1948 their plan to make West Germany independent annoyed the Russians, who retaliated by stopping all traffic between West Germany and West Berlin. The Allies kept West Berlin supplied with food, clothing, even coal, by air alone, flying in 6,000 tonnes a day. The Russians did not try to stop the flights and, after 15 months, reopened the road.

The Cold War

Members of the UN fell into two groups: the Communist or Eastern bloc, led by the Soviet Union, and the capitalist or Western bloc, led by the USA. As more countries, many of them former colonies, joined, a third bloc developed, sometimes known as the Third World.

The USA and the Soviet Union were the strongest powers in 1945. US troops remained in western Europe and US aid poured into Europe to help revive countries ruined by the war. The Soviet Union had gained an 'empire' of dependent states in eastern Europe, including East Germany. These countries had their own communist governments, but took orders from Russia. From the 1947 to the 1970s the world was shaken by a series of crises resulting from the 'Cold War' between the USA and the Soviet Union – and later, Communist China. At times, another world war looked likely.

Cuba

Fidel Castro's revolution in Cuba (1956) established a communist government, supported by the Soviet Union, in 'America's backyard'. In 1962, another world crisis erupted when US spy planes discovered Soviet nuclear missiles in Cuba. US president John F. Kennedy demanded their removal. After a few days when nuclear war seemed possible, the Russians agreed.

The European Economic Community

Groups of countries formed their own international associations. Often the reasons were economic – to increase trade and business by ending customs duties and agreeing to common rules. The European Economic Community was formed in 1957 by six Western European countries, later joined by most others. In 1991 it became the European Union.

The Middle East since 1945

The Middle East has been the world's most troubled region since 1945. The creation of a Jewish state, Israel, in the Arab land of Palestine was the main cause of wars. There have also been other wars. Other countries, especially in the West, were worried by these wars because the Middle East contains the world's main supply of oil.

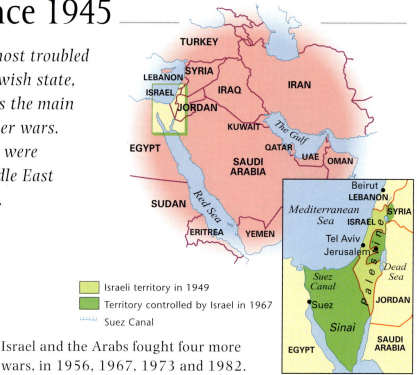

Israeli territory in 1949

Territory controlled by Israel in 1967

Suez Canal

Arabs and Israelis

Since the early 20th century Jews had settled in Arab Palestine, their ancient homeland. This increased after the Second World War. Although the Arabs protested, in 1947 the United Nations voted to divide Palestine into separate Jewish and Arab provinces. The next year, the Jews declared Israel a republic. Their Arab neighbours at once attacked, but Israel, supported by the USA, won.

Israel and the Arabs fought four more wars, in 1956, 1967, 1973 and 1982. In 1967 Israel captured much Arab land. It kept some of this land, including the Arab part of Palestine called the Occupied Territories.

▽ A Palestinian refugee camp in Lebanon, in 1982.

The Palestinians

The Palestinians had no country. Some lived in Israel and the Occupied Territories, some in other Arab countries. Some Palestinians formed the Palestine Liberation Organisation to fight for an Arab state. After a rebellion by Palestinians in the Occupied Territories, Israel was forced to make an agreement with Palestinian leader Yasser Arafat (1993). It gave the Palestinians some control of the Occupied Territories. The two sides quarrelled over who should control Jerusalem and fighting began again.

Gamal Abdel Nasser

Many of the newly independent Arab states after 1945 were led by strong nationalists. They were often army officers. The greatest was Gamal Abdel Nasser, who gained power in Egypt in 1954. He led Arab opposition against Israel and against Western influence.

The Suez Crisis

In 1956 Egypt's President Nasser took over the Suez Canal, which was owned by Europeans. When talks failed, British and French troops landed in the Canal Zone, and Israel attacked Egypt overland. The whole world was shocked. The invading troops were forced to withdraw, leaving Nasser victorious.

Iran

In Iran an old-fashioned religious leader, the Ayatollah Khomeini, came to power after a revolution in 1979. He made Iran a much stricter Muslim country, governed by religious law. Women could not have jobs and had to wear veils in public.

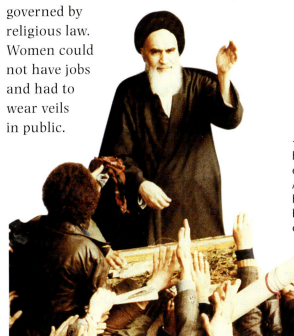

◁ Ayatollah Khomeini hated the West, especially the Americans. He and his supporters believed that Western civilisation was evil.

Oil

Oil exports made many Middle Eastern states around the Persian Gulf very rich. The greatest oil producer in the region was Saudi Arabia. Western countries needed that oil, and were therefore interested in Middle Eastern affairs. The USA feared that, if Iraq controlled the Gulf, the oil supply would be stopped.

Iraq – a dangerous neighbour

The military dictator of Iraq, Saddam Hussein, took advantage of the chaos in Iran by invading it. He was afraid that Khomeini's revolution might spread to Iraq. He also wanted to control the entrance to the Persian Gulf, then shared with Iran. The Iran-Iraq war lasted eight years (1980-88), and about 1 million people were killed. In 1990 Saddam invaded a smaller neighbour on the Gulf, Kuwait. In 1991 the forces of the United Nations, led by the USA and supported by many other countries including some Arab states, soon forced Saddam's army out. Saddam remained in power, and small clashes continued.

△ Saddam Hussein

Asia since 1945

South-east Asia was another troubled region in the late 20th century. Besides the two superpowers, China was a powerful force in the region. So was Japan, as it built up its industries after the disasters of the war.

The Korean War

After the Second World War, Korea, freed from Japanese occupation was divided into two – communist North Korea, supported by the Soviet Union, and capitalist South Korea, supported by the USA. In 1950, North Korea invaded the South. A UN force, led by the USA, was sent to defend the South, and Chinese forces fought for the North. A truce was agreed in 1953, leaving Korea divided.

China

In the Chinese republic, nationalists and communists had fought together against the Japanese. But when peace came, their alliance ended and civil war began again. Mao Zedong led the communists to victory and drove the nationalists out of China. With US support, nationalists set up their own state on the island of Taiwan and claimed to be the rightful government of China. The Chinese communists had Soviet support, but the two countries later quarrelled. After 1960, Mao's China was no more friendly to the Soviet Union than it was to the USA.

The main task of the new regime was to modernise the country. They reorganised farming on the communist pattern (no private land), and started developing industry. Progess was far from smooth. Mao's policies caused distress and chaos, especially the attacks on middle-class people during what was called the Cultural Revolution (1966-69). Communist China was also active in foreign affairs. Its conquest of Tibet (1951), which it insisted was part of the Chinese empire, caused a short border war with India.

▽ The world was shocked when Chinese troops killed 1,000 peaceful demonstrators in Tiananmen Square, Beijing, in 1989. The demonstrators, mostly students, were demanding greater democracy. After 1989 the government still kept tight control over the people, but it allowed far more freedom to business and industry.

South-east Asia

Vietnam, like Korea, was divided into a communist North, led by Ho Chi Minh, and a capitalist South, supported by the USA. The USA provided military aid to prevent South Vietnam being taken over by the communists. By the mid-1960s, the USA was fighting a major war against the Vietnamese communists. The war was extremely unpopular with Americans and in 1973 the American forces withdrew. It was the first time the USA had been defeated in war. The communists took over the whole of Vietnam.

△ When North Vietnam conquered the South, thousands of people tried to escape by boat to Hong Kong.

In 1976 Cambodia fell under the control of the Khmer Rouge, an extreme revolutionary movement led by Pol Pot. Millions of ordinary Cambodians died in Pol Pot's reign of terror until a Vietnamese invasion overthrew him in 1979.

▽ Although they had few natural resources, the Japanese were expert in making things. They bought cheap raw materials to make expensive products. In Tokyo, prosperity brought traffic jams.

New Asian states

The new states created from former European colonies suffered some of the problems of other 'Third World' countries in Africa and Latin America, including poverty. Most called themselves democracies, but power and wealth remained in the hands of small groups, often dominated by generals. Indonesia (the third largest Asian country after China and India), Pakistan and Myanmar (Burma) were all ruled for long periods by military dictators, who had little respect for human rights. Afghanistan was ruined by endless civil wars that began with Soviet occupation in 1979-89. Other Far Eastern states, such as Malaysia, Singapore, South Korea, even Indonesia, made great progress in industry and business. By the 1980s they challenged the West. But some were troubled by social problems, failing businesses and the threat of revolution.

Japan

The greatest success story in Asia came from Japan. Supported by the USA, Japan became a peaceful, modern and wealthy republic. By the 1980s it was the richest country in the world after the USA. Some other countries followed Japan's example. Hong Kong, a British colony that was returned to China in 1997, was a world centre of business.

Human Rights

Most governments accepted that everyone has rights, such as the freedom to say and believe what they like, although some still ruled by force and fear. At the same time, old divisions of race, class, sex, religion or other differences, though still violent in some countries, became less sharp.

▽ Martin Luther King Jr (1929-68) leading a civil-rights march in Washington, the US capital. He was a Baptist minister from the American South, whose passionate speeches and brave policy of non-violence made him leader of the US civil rights movement. He was murdered, aged 39, by a white racist.

Civil Rights

In the USA, all citizens were supposed to be free and equal. But black people, who made up 15 per cent of the population, suffered from race prejudice. In some Southern states, blacks were prevented from voting in elections. They had separate (and worse) schools, hospitals, even public toilets. In the North there was no official separation, but many blacks lived in all-black slums and could not get good jobs.

The rise of the civil rights movement in the 1950s forced the government to pass new laws to make sure that blacks got equal treatment. The greatest civil-rights leader was Martin Luther King Jr. He learned from Gandhi in India that peaceful protest is a less harmful way to bring about change than violent revolution. The new laws did not bring prosperity to all blacks or change the black slums in many cities. They did not end racial prejudice, as people always find reasons to hate neighbours who are 'different'. But blacks could live and work where they liked, and race relations did improve.

Political freedom

Many other Western countries contained racial minorities which, from about 1960, also won equal rights and opportunities. In Australia and New Zealand, the rights of Aborigines and Maoris were recognised at last. They even regained some of the lands that early white colonists had taken. Multi-racial societies developed in European countries such as Britain and France, which gained many immigrants from former Asian and African colonies. But in countries such as South Africa, although the ruling whites were a minority, blacks and 'coloured' people were third-class citizens.

Women

The civil rights movement strengthened the cause of women's rights. Even in democratic countries, women did not gain the vote until the early 20th century. In other ways they were still far from equal with men. In 1950 it was still difficult for a woman to go to university, to own property, or work in business and professions such as law and medicine. Only the Soviet Union and other communist countries had laws that made women equal with men. The idea that a woman's place is in the home was still common. To win equal rights, women needed not only new laws but new customs, which cannot be changed so easily. Women campaigned against sex discrimination at work and at home, and for the right to equal pay, as they were often paid less than men for the same work.

▷ Building surveyors in Bangladesh. Twenty years previously, no woman could have held such a job.

Rich and poor

Besides blacks and women, most minority groups in the West gained fairer treatment between 1950 and 2000. This was made easier by growing wealth. International industry and business, aided by amazing advances in science and technology, made most people better off. But the growing wealth mainly affected countries in the northern part of the world – North America, Europe and Japan – plus Australia and New Zealand. In the poorer countries of South America and Africa, and many parts of Asia, the standard of living of most people rose only a little, if at all. In 1983, the average income of someone in the USA or France was over $10,000 a year, but in many African countries it was less than $200.

Wealth also means health. Poor countries could not afford many doctors, decent houses, and clean water supplies. So people often died young. The average lifetime of a woman in central Africa was under 50 years. In Japan it was 78 years.

△ Women making baskets. Simple crafts like this were for centuries the only work for many people. In 2000 the gap between rich and poor was still huge. The world's wealth was still shared unfairly – a great problem for the future.

Science and Health

Between 1950 and 2000 the living standards of most people in the industrial countries improved. That was made possible by advances in technology, science and medicine. But some people feared that such progress could not go on for ever.

Fossil fuel

Industrial peoples need two things from Nature: the raw materials to make things, and the power to drive their machines. In the Industrial Revolution, power came from burning coal. After 1950, oil became the chief industrial fuel. Both coal and oil are fossil fuels, formed in the Earth over millions of years. In the 1970s people feared that supplies of oil would run out in a few years. Their fears ended when new deposits of oil and gas were found, some under the seas. But the need to find new kinds of power continued.

Nuclear power

Nuclear fission, which produced the atom bomb, could also be used to provide power. In the 1950s, many people believed nuclear power would replace fossil fuels. But the dangers were too great. After an explosion in a nuclear power station in Chernobyl, Ukraine, in 1986, few new ones were built.

Science

More universities produced more scientists. New discoveries and inventions led to astonishing advances in most kinds of science, from astronomy to zoology. The history of the Earth and the universe became clearer. Proof that the surface of the Earth rests on slowly moving 'plates' showed how the oceans and continents had formed. Advances in electronics caused big changes in many human activities, in work and play. In about 1960 lasers were invented to produce a very precise beam of light. They proved useful in many ways, from making pictures in three dimensions (called holographs) to slowing down atoms to make them easier to study. Some scientists believed that lasers might one day be used to control nuclear fusion, which would solve the energy problem.

▽ The success of medical engineers in making tiny surgical tools allowed doctors to see inside a patient without making a large cut. Here, a tiny camera on the end of a thin, bendy tube takes pictures of the blood flowing round the body, and sends them to the monitor.

Medicine

Lasers were also useful in surgery. For instance, surgeons sometimes used their precise beam to 'burn' out a growth like a cancer. Another spectacular advance in surgery was transplanting living organs. In 1967 a South African surgeon, Christiaan Barnard, carried out the first transplant of a human heart.

Expensive surgical operations affected only a few people, but medical researchers also had many successes in fighting infectious disease. Smallpox disappeared by 1979, thanks to the efforts of the World Heath Organization. New vaccines prevented other killer diseases, such as polio (poliomyelitis). New drugs, such as antibiotics, brought cures for other diseases. New treatments made some kinds of cancer less deadly. However, new diseases, such as AIDS, also appeared, and some that had been largely conquered, such as TB (tuberculosis), started to increase again.

◁ Experiments with the power of the Sun, wind and ocean tides provided 'alternative' energy. This wind farm supplied energy for a small town, but required a large space, damaged wild life and looked ugly.

Genetics

Perhaps the most extraordinary advance was in genetics, the discovery of how the characteristics of a living thing are inherited through its genes. With this knowledge, crops could be altered, to make them bigger or to give them defence against disease. By 2001 genetic engineering could prevent some heriditary diseases. It was also possible to 'design' a child (its hair colour, whether it was a girl or boy etc) before it was born.

Dolly the sheep

She looks like an ordinary sheep, but Dolly has no proper parents. She was 'grown' in a Scottish lab from a single cell of a six-year-old ewe in 1996. Because she has exactly the same genes as that ewe, she is a 'clone', a perfect copy. But Dolly raised questions. How old would she be in 2000? Four – or ten? More serious: would the next step be an artificial human being? These experiments with nature worried many people.

People and the Planet

In the late 20th century many people were worried that human beings were seriously damaging their planet. There were two main problems. The first was the growth in world population. The second was pollution.

Population explosion

Ten thousand years ago, the world contained about 10 million people. By 1650 there were 500 million, by 1930 2 billion, and by 2000 about 6 billion. Not only did the population constantly increase, the rate at which it grew also increased. About three-quarters of the world's population lived in the poorer 'Third World' countries, where the rate of growth was highest. The rising population in those countries made it difficult to raise the standard of living, as populations tended to grow as fast or faster than the nation's wealth.

In richer countries, population grew more slowly because many people practised birth control, so families had fewer children. But poor countries could not afford birth-control programmes, and poor families often want lots of children. Some religions taught that birth control is wrong. China, which had the world's largest population, passed a law to stop any married couple having more than one child. But such extreme methods could be used only where the government had absolute power.

▷ The rising population was one of many causes of worldwide worries about the environment. In parts of Africa, good soil was worn out by too much use. In tropical countries, valuable forest was cut down for farmland.

The environment

Serious pollution of the Earth began in the Industrial Revolution, but the effects were not seen for many years. Not until the 1980s did ordinary people begin to fear that the planet was being ruined. Natural resources were being used up at a dangerous rate – not only fossil fuels but forests, fish, even fresh water. Many plants and animals were becoming extinct. Little true wilderness was left on Earth.

Factories and machines poured dangerous gases into the air. In Scandinavia, trees died and lakes were poisoned by 'acid rain', formed when industrial chemicals are dissolved in rain drops. Human waste was pumped into the sea, and oil spilled from giant tankers killed sea life.

▽ In rich countries, people produced more and more rubbish, as everything became highly packaged. In poor countries, people would pick through a rubbish dump, looking for anything to sell, or to eat.

Climate

By 2000 most scientists agreed that the Earth's climate was getting warmer. Even a rise of only 2°C over the next 50 years would ruin many farmers and melt ice in polar regions, causing huge floods. The warmer climate was blamed on the 'greenhouse effect', caused by industrial gases that form a kind of blanket around the Earth, keeping it warm.

Changes were also noticed in the atmosphere. The ozone layer, which protects the Earth from the Sun's harmful ultraviolet rays, was thinner. The main cause was traced to man-made chemicals called chlorofluorocarbons (CFCs).

▷ Human beings have been cutting down the forests for hundreds of years. In the late 20th century thousands of hectares of rain forest were destroyed every year by timber companies, miners and farmers. They contained many unknown plants and animals. In the past, new medicines have come from rain-forest plants.

The Rainbow Warrior

The Rainbow Warrior belonged to the environmental group Greenpeace. It was blown up in New Zealand by French secret agents in 1985 to prevent it interfering in tests of nuclear weapons in the Pacific. Greenpeace, founded in 1971, was one of the liveliest of many international charities working for the environment.

Conservation

In 1990 most countries agreed to stop using CFCs. In 1992 an international conference on the environment showed that the whole world was worried about pollution. Governments promised to reduce the harmful effects of their industries, to protect fishing, and reduce fumes from vehicles and factories. But the problems were not easy to solve, because the solutions were expensive. The poor countries did not want to stop industrial development just to preserve the natural environment. The rich countries did not want to reduce their standard of living by expensive methods of controlling pollution.

A Small World

By 2000 the world seemed a small place. People travelled more. News and pictures were broadcast round the world in seconds. Someone with a computer linked to the Internet could exchange information with almost anyone, anywhere.

◁ Dealers in stocks and shares can see how prices are changing in stock markets all over the world at any one moment.

International business

Agreement on customs duties and international associations such as the European Union or OPEC (Oil Producing and Exporting Countries) helped the growth of world trade. Business became international. Large companies had offices, factories and shareholders in many countries. A German car might have parts made in France, Britain and Japan. Large companies bought rival firms in foreign countries. Cities around the world looked more alike. Businessmen in Frankfurt and Tokyo wore the same kind of suits and worked in similar offices. They often spoke the same language, English, which was becoming an international language.

Transport

Air travel became quicker and cheaper as more people spent holidays abroad. Huge improvements in surface transport included a tunnel under the English Channel and a 2,000-metre bridge joining two of Japan's islands. Increasing trade and more car-owning families increased road traffic by millions of vehicles. More leisure time and more money meant people could afford to travel abroad more often, and further than ever before. By 2000 tourists could visit the most remote places on Earth.

Boeing 247D, 1933

Concorde, 1970

The Challenger, c. 1880

Maglev train, 2000

Space

The space age began in 1961 when a Russian, Yuri Gagarin, circled the Earth in Sputnik I. In 1969 Americans landed on the Moon. In the 1970s the Russians developed the space lab, where several scientists could work in space for months.

The Americans invented the space 'shuttle' (1981), part spacecraft, part airplane, which could be used many times. Unmanned spacecraft explored the planets and beyond. By 2000 hundreds of man-made satellites were circling the Earth. Some were for scientific research, providing new knowledge of the Earth and tracking weather systems. Many were for communications, sending TV and other signals around the world. The American Hubble telescope scanned the universe from Earth orbit.

▷ US astronaut Bruce McCandless tested a Manned Manoeuvering Unit from the Space Shuttle in 1984. This device allows an astronaut to move about freely in space.

△ Computers entered schools and homes, as well as offices, when PCs (personal computers) were developed in the 1970s.

The communications revolution

Of all the technological changes of 1950-2000, the most important were in electronic communications. They affected everyone in the world, bringing some problems as well as great benefits. The first computers were developed to decipher enemy radio messages during the Second World War. They were really just huge calculating machines. The first one, called Colossus, weighed over a tonne but was far less powerful than a modern laptop. By the 1980s, most businesses and many homes used computers. New developments such as fax, e-mail and the Internet followed, along with video recorders and cameras, mobile telephones and digital TV. In 1971 the invention of the 'microprocessor', needing only one small silicon chip, resulted in smaller, cheaper computers. The personal computer (PC) followed. The computer business itself created many new industries to produce computer equipment.

The End of the Century

The main event of the last years of the 20th century was the collapse of the Communist system in Europe, beginning in 1989. In other parts of the world too, governments that had relied on force to keep them in power disappeared. Democracy took a step forward.

The end of the Soviet Union

Communism had dominated the Soviet Union, the world's largest country, since 1917. Since the 1940s the Soviet Union had also controlled more than half of Europe and much of central Asia. In 1985 Mikhail Gorbachev became Soviet leader. He was a bold reformer. He introduced new policies to give people more freedom, and was willing to listen to those who disagreed with him. Political prisoners were set free. Gorbachev also wanted a complete change in foreign policy, involving international cooperation, instead of competition. This meant ending the Cold War, which was not too difficult as the US government and its allies also wanted to end it.

Giving people more freedom was easy too, but it was also dangerous. By reducing the power of the Communist Party, Gorbachev gave the nations in the Soviet Union, and other states of Eastern Europe under communist rule, the chance to get rid of Soviet control and communist governments. The huge Soviet empire suddenly broke up, as countries elected democratic governments. The Communist Party was banned in Russia in 1991 and the Soviet Union officially ended. But without the Party system, the government was weak. Crime increased and living standards fell even further below the standards of the West.

▷ Nelson Mandela welcomed by his supporters after his release from prison. Between them, he and De Klerk made South Africa a democracy.

▽ East Germans rejoicing at the demolition of the Berlin Wall, in November 1989. The Wall was built in 1961 to stop people escaping to the West. As the communist government of East Germany collapsed, thousands of people left for the West. In 1990 the two Germanies were reunited as one country.

South Africa

With its racist policy of apartheid, South Africa was an outcast among other countries. Some reforms were made before F. W. de Klerk, South Africa's Gorbachev, became president in 1989. Supported by most whites as well as others, he promised to end apartheid. In 1990, the African National Congress, the banned black nationalist party, was legalised. The ANC's veteran leader, Nelson Mandela, was released from prison after 26 years. South Africa ended the apartheid laws (1991) and held the first fully democratic elections in 1994. The ANC won a majority and Mandela, a popular hero throughout the world, became the first black president of the 'rainbow nation' (people of all colours).

Latin America

After gaining independence, most Latin American countries suffered from unstable, unjust governments and crude military dictators, sometimes supported by the USA. Bolivia had 180 rebellions between 1825 and 1952. About 100,000 Guatemalans died by violence between the 1960s and 1980s. But by the 1990s, reforms and democracy brought better times to many countries. Dictators, some of them mass murderers, were overthrown in Argentina (1983), Brazil (1985), Chile, Paraguay and – by US forces – in Panama (1989). Long and murderous civil wars ended in Nicaragua (1990), El Salvador and Guatemala (1992) The countries set up more just and more democratic governments. Huge human problems remained, especially the terrible poverty of the big-city slums.

△ Rigoberta Menchú Tum of Guatemala receives her Nobel Peace Prize in 1992. It was awarded for her campaigning for human rights, especially for indigenous peoples.

The world at the end of the 20th century

In 2000, human beings could look back at the most violent century in their history. It had more wars, with more people killed, and more brutal governments, than any earlier century. However, there was no big international war after 1945, and few people expected a world war in the future.

It was also a century of great achievements and, in spite of so much violence and cruelty, the future looked better than the past. Most people, though not all, were better off by 2000. Famine and disease had not ended, but they were less common. Science and medicine had made amazing advances. Perhaps the most important change was that many nations and people had grown more tolerant. Through the UN and other organisations, nations were more willing to help others. More people recognised that every human being has rights. They were learning to live peacefully with others of different ethnic background, class, or gender.

The 20th-Century World

Two terrible world wars were fought in the first half of the century. After 1945, the year of the atomic bomb, world statesmen founded the United Nations, to prevent another world war. At the same time, the West began to see that freedom and equality should be for

AMERICAS

1900-1916
1903 The Wright brothers make the first flight in a petrol-engined aircraft, in North Carolina.
1911 The Mexican Revolution begins.
1911 The first film studio opens in Hollywood, California.
1914 The Panama Canal opens, linking the Atlantic and Pacific Oceans.

1917-1933
1917 The USA enters the First World War against Germany.
1928 The first Mickey Mouse cartoon film is made. The movie industry flourishes (right).
1929 A stock market slump causes a worldwide economic depression.
1931 Canada becomes an independent nation.

1934-1949
1936 The African-American Jesse Owens wins four gold medals at the Berlin Olympic Games.
1941 The USA enters the Second World War, after a Japanese attack on Pearl Harbor.
1944 Juan Perón comes to power in Argentina.
1945 The United Nations headquarters is established in New York.

EUROPE

1900-1916
1905 Norway becomes independent from Sweden.
1906 In Finland women win the right to vote.
1908 Bulgaria declares independence from the Ottoman Empire.
1909 Frenchman Louis Blériot makes the first aeroplane flight across the English Channel.
1914 The First World War begins.

1917-1933
1917 The Russian revolution begins in March. The Bolsheviks take over Russia in November.
1919 The peace treaty to end the First World War is signed at Versailles.
1919 Millions die in a flu epidemic.
1920 The League of Nations is founded. It fails to stop attacks by one country on another.
1922 The Irish Free State (Eire) becomes largely independent of Britain.
1922 Mussolini gains power in Italy.
1933 Hitler becomes chancellor of Germany.

1934-1949
1936 Civil war breaks out in Spain.
1936 Volkswagen begins making the 'Beetle' car (below).
1939 The Second World War begins after Hitler invades Poland.
1941 Germany invades Russia.
1945 The Second World War ends with the defeat of Germany and Japan.
1948 Communists take over in Eastern European countries.

ASIA and OCEANIA

1900-1916
1900 The Boxer Rebellion against foreigners breaks out in China (left).
1904 War begins between Russia and Japan. Russia is defeated in 1905.
1911 China becomes a republic after a revolution.
1913 Indian poet Rabindranath Tagore wins the Nobel Prize for Literature.

1917-1933
1918 Queen Salote becomes queen of Tonga. She rules for 47 years.
1927 Canberra becomes the federal capital of Australia.
1931 New Zealand becomes an independent nation.
1931 The Japanese take over Manchuria.

1934-1949
1935 The first Labour government is elected in New Zealand.
1942 Japan completes its conquest of south-east Asia and Indonesia.
1945 Japan surrenders after US aircraft drop atom bombs (left) on the cities of Hiroshima and Nagasaki.
1947 India and Pakistan gain independence from Britain.
1949 Indonesia gains independence. Communists, led by Mao Zedong, defeat nationalists in the Chinese civil war.

AFRICA and MIDDLE EAST

1900-1916
1910 The Union of South Africa is created.
1911 Italy invades Libya.
1912 The African National Congress is founded, to promote the rights of Africans in a country dominated by a European minority.

1917-1933
1918 Conflicts begin between the immigrant Jews and the Arabs in Palestine.
1922 Turkey becomes a republic.
1926 The Moroccan rebellion is defeated by Spain and France.
1930 Haile Selassie becomes emperor of Ethiopia. This cross (left) is from Ethiopia.
1932 Ibn Saud creates the kingdom of Saudi Arabia.

1934-1949
1935 Italy invades and takes control of Ethiopia.
1942 At the Battle of El Alamein in Egypt the Allies defeat the Germans.
1945 The formation of the Arab League, in Cairo.
1948 The state of Israel is founded, leading to the first Arab-Israeli war.
1949 The South African government introduces apartheid.

everyone, and European empires came to an end. That led also to greater equality among people of different race, religion and gender. Of course wars, violence and prejudice continued, but after over 2000 years of conflict the peoples of the world were coming closer together.

1950-1966	1967-1982	1983-2000
1955 President Perón is overthrown in Argentina. **1959** Hawaii becomes the 50th state of the USA. **1963** US President John F. Kennedy (right) is assassinated in Texas. **1965** America enters the conflict in Vietnam.	**1968** The black civil rights leader Martin Luther King is assassinated. **1969** US astronaut Neil Armstrong becomes the first person on the Moon (right). **1973** President Allende of Chile is overthrown in a military revolt led by Pinochet. **1974** US President Nixon is forced to resign after the 'Watergate' scandal.	**1983** A communist coup in Grenada is defeated by US invasion. **1992** A 12-year-old civil war ends in El Salvador. **1992** An international 'Earth summit' is held at Rio de Janeiro to discuss problems of the environment.

1951 The first nuclear power stations are built. **1956** Soviet tanks crush an anti-communist revolt in Hungary. **1957** The European Community is founded. **1957** Russia launches the first space satellite, Sputnik I. **1961** The Russian Yuri Gagarin becomes the first person to travel in space.	**1968** The liberal government in Czechoslovakia is overthrown by Soviet invasion. **1969** The IRA begins fighting for a united Ireland. **1973** Greece becomes a republic. **1975** The monarchy is restored in Spain. **1980** The Polish trade union, Solidarity, is founded (left) and opposes the Soviet-controlled communist government. 	**1989** Demonstrations force communists from power in East European states. **1991** Wars break out in the Balkans, as Yugoslavia splits into separate states. **1991** Gorbachev resigns and the Communist Party is banned in Russia. **1995** A peace agreement ends the civil war in Bosnia. **1999** NATO forces attack the Serbs over their treatment of Albanians in Kosovo. **1999** The European Union introduces a single currency, the Euro.

1950 The Korean War breaks out. **1953** Hillary and Tensing reach the top of Mount Everest (right). **1957** Civil war begins in Vietnam. **1962** A border war breaks out between China and India. **1966** The Cultural Revolution begins in China.	**1971** Bangladesh gains independence from Pakistan. **1973** The last US troops leave Vietnam. **1975** Pol Pot gains power in Cambodia, and communists control Laos and Vietnam. **1975** Papua New Guinea gains independence from Australia.	**1984** The Indian prime minister Indira Gandhi (left) is assassinated. **1986** The South Pacific Nuclear-Free Zone is set up. **1989** Chinese government forces massacre student protesters in Tiananmen Square. **1991** Indian Prime Minister Rajiv Gandhi (son of Indira) is assassinated. **1997** Britain returns Hong Kong to China. **1998** Riots in Indonesia force the country's military leader, Suharto, to resign.

1957 Nkrumah (right) leads Ghana to independence. **1957** France and Britain begin to withdraw from their colonies. **1962** Algeria gains independence from France. **1965** Rhodesia declares its independence from Britain. 	**1967** Biafra withdraws from the federation of Nigeria, causing civil war. **1975** Angola and Mozambique gain independence from Portugal. **1979** Ayatollah Khomeini gains power in Iran. Soviet forces invade Afghanistan. **1980** The Iraq-Iran war begins. **1982** Israel invades Lebanon.	**1984** About 1 million people die of starvation and disease in an Ethiopian famine. **1991** US-led forces drive Iraqi invaders from Kuwait. **1993** Arab and Israeli leaders sign a declaration to promote a settlement of their conflict in Palestine. **1994** About 1 million die in civil war in Rwanda. Mandela becomes President of South Africa after the first ever multi-racial election.

Who's Who

Castro, Fidel (born 1927), Cuban leader. He led a popular revolution against the Cuban dictator, Batista, in 1958, and turned Cuba into a communist state, supported by the Soviet Union. In spite of US efforts to get rid of him, he stayed in power even after the collapse of the Soviet Union in 1989.

Churchill, Sir Winston (1874-1965), British statesman. He first entered parliament in 1874 and had an up-and-down career until he became prime minister in 1940. He led Britain throughout the Second World War with great heart and skill, inspiring people with his fighting speeches and planning the strategy that brought victory.

De Gaulle, Charles (1898-1970), French statesman. An army general, he escaped to Britain when France was conquered in 1940, and became the leader of the Free French, uniting all those who opposed the German occupation. He was president of France in 1944-46, and in 1959-69, granting independence to Algeria in 1962.

Ford, Henry (1863-1947), US engineer and businessman. He designed cars and founded a company in Detroit (1903) to produce them. They were the first to be mass-produced on an assembly line. Though he paid high wages, his Model T ('Tin Lizzie') was cheap enough for ordinary families to buy – 15 million were sold.

Franco, General Francisco (1892-1975), Spanish dictator. He was a leader of the revolt that led to the Spanish Civil War. From 1939 he governed Spain as a police state. Though friendly to Hitler, he kept Spain out of the Second World War. Afterwards, his hatred of communism gained him some support from the USA.

Gandhi, Indira (1917-84), prime minister of India. Daughter of Jawaharlal Nehru, she followed him as prime minister in 1966 and dominated Indian affairs for 20 years. She lost power in 1977 and was accused of undemocratic government, but won again in 1980. Like her namesake, M. K. Gandhi, she was murdered.

Gandhi, Mohandas K. (1869-1948), Indian leader. As a lawyer in South Africa until 1914, he worked bravely against racist laws. In India he became leader of the National Congress and worked for independence from Britain by non-violent protest. His efforts to make peace between Hindus and Muslims led to his murder by a Hindu extremist.

Gorbachev, Mikhail (born 1931), last leader of the Soviet Union. He worked his way up through the Communist Party and was chosen as leader in 1985. His reforms, which were meant to bring peace, freedom and better living, led to the break-up of the Soviet Union and the collapse of the communist system in Europe.

Hitler, Adolf (1889-1945), German dictator. A soldier in 1914-18, he became leader of the National Socialist (Nazi) Party. In prison in 1923 he wrote *Mein Kampf* ('My Struggle'), an attack on Germany's supposed enemies, including Jews. Gaining power in 1933, he made Germany a police state and provoked the Second World War.

King, Martin Luther (1929-68), the greatest US civil-rights leader. As a black minister of the Baptist Church in racist Alabama, he was a founder and later leader of the Southern Christian Leadership Conference, which fought for racial equality by the methods of Gandhi. An inspiring speaker, he was assassinated by a white racist.

Lenin real name V. I. Ulyanov (1870-1924), first leader of the Soviet Union. A Marxist and a rebel, often in prison or exile, he led the Bosheviks in the Russian Revolution (1917), and planned the communist system. His policies were brutal, but the worst atrocities of communist rule happened under his successor, Stalin.

Mandela, Nelson (born 1918), South African statesman. He joined the African National Congress in 1944 and led opposition to the racist policy of apartheid. From 1964 to 1990 he was in prison, but when apartheid ended he was elected the first black South African president (1991). He was admired everywhere for his tolerance.

Mao Zedong (1893-1976), Chinese communist leader. He was one of the founders of the Chinese Communist Party, and led the country after the Revolution (1949). His rule was intolerant, his policies often unwise: his 'Great Leap Forward' (1958) was a leap back. After that his influence later faded, but no one dared to criticise him.

Mussolini, Benito (1883-1945), Italian fascist leader. A socialist in his youth, he founded the fascist movement in 1919, became prime minister in 1922, and made himself a dictator. An extreme nationalist, he believed in force rather than law. He invaded Ethiopia and, as Hitler's ally, led Italy into war. He was overthrown in 1943.

Nasser, Gamal Abdel (1918-70), Egyptian president. After a military revolt against the King of Egypt, Colonel Nasser became leader. He caused a world crisis by taking over the Suez Canal (1956), and was defeated by Israel in the Six-Day War (1967), but was recognised as the greatest Arab leader in the Middle East.

Roosevelt, Eleanor (1882-1962), worker for human rights. The wife of President Franklin Roosevelt, she strongly supported civil rights for blacks and for women. After her husband's death she became a delegate to the newly formed United Nations, and headed the UN Human Rights Commission (1947-51).

Roosevelt, Franklin D. (1882-1945), US statesman, the only president to have served more than eight years (1933-45). He is remembered most for his 'New Deal' policies in the 1930s, which tried to end the depression by government action, and for his leadership during the Second World War, in close alliance with Churchill.

Stalin real name Iosiph Dzugashvili (1879-1953), dictator of the Soviet Union. He took part in the Bolshevik Revolution (1917) and succeeded Lenin as leader in 1924. He got rid of all opponents, real or imaginary, caused the death or exile of millions of people, but gained credit from the defeat of Germany (1943-45).

Glossary

absolute ruler A king or other ruler whose power is not limited by laws.

allies Countries, or other groups, who join together for some cause, especially in war.

apartheid The system of laws of the government in South Africa from 1948 to 1991. It divided people into racial groups and gave more rights and better services to white people.

artillery Large guns firing cannon balls or, in later times, explosives.

assembly line A method of production in factories, when the thing being made passes from one group of workers to another. Each group completes one step in the process.

Axis The alliance of Germany, Italy and, later, Japan during the Second World War.

blitzkreig German for 'lightning war', the speedy form of attack, with tanks and aircraft, that German armies made in the Second World War.

Bolsheviks The revolutionary group in Russia who carried out the revolution of November 1917.

broadcasting Sending messages in sound and vision by radio waves, which are picked up by radio and TV receivers.

collectivism A system where a group of people share ownership of the land and the means of production, such as factories.

colony A settlement of people in another country or a country that is ruled by another one.

communism An extreme form of socialism, in which all power and property belongs to the state, and the state is run by a single party.

conscription A system in which all people able to fight have to serve in the armed forces.

coup Short for coup d'état. The sudden overthrow of a government, usually by a person or persons who hold some power in the state.

Cultural Revolution The policy of the government of Mao Zedong in communist China in 1966-69. It was an attempt to continue the spirit of Mao's communist revolution, using gangs of youths called Red Guards, but it ended in violence and economic upheaval.

customs duties Taxes on goods coming into a country.

democracy A country or form of government where power depends on the votes of the people.

dictator A ruler with absolute power, often gained illegally, for instance by a coup d'état.

discrimination Unfair treatment of a group of people because of their religion, ethnic group, sex, or for some other cause that makes them different from the rest.

economy The management of the whole wealth of a state (or another type of community), including money, trade, and industry.

emancipation Freedom from some kind of unfair treatment, such as freedom from slavery, or the gaining of a right, such as the right to vote.

empire A state which also controls other peoples or states.

fascism An extreme form of government, under a dictator. Fascism puts the interests of the state before the interests of the citizen, and depends more on force than on law.

finance The management of all money matters.

genetic engineering Changing the nature of a living thing by altering its genes, which carry the 'instructions' controlling its character.

immigrants People who have settled in a foreign country, often because of persecution in their own country.

Latin America The countries of Mexico and Central and South America, where Spanish or Portuguese are spoken.

liberalism Political opinion in favour of reform and greater freedom.

mercenary A professional soldier, willing to fight for anyone who pays him.

Glossary

Middle East   The region of south-west Asia from the Mediterranean to Afghanistan.

militia   An armed force. Unlike an army, a militia is a local group of part-time soldiers, who are called up in an emergency, such as a rebellion.

Modern style   A general name for the big changes in style of art, architecture and literature that occurred in the early 20th century.

mutiny   A rebellion by soldiers or sailors.

nationalisation   Placing industries (or land, or institutions) under the control of the government. This was usually the policy of socialist governments.

nationalism   Support for the idea of the nation, especially in a nation that is ruled by another power.

Nazis   Members of the National Socialist German Workers' party, which gained power under Hitler in 1933.

Near East   The region around the eastern Mediterranean, sometimes including Egypt and south-east Europe. Like 'Middle East', the name has no exact meaning.

nuclear weapons   Powerful weapons whose explosions are caused by the process of nuclear fission or nuclear fusion.

parliament   A government assembly, made up of people elected by the citizens. In modern democratic countries, parliament is often the body that makes the laws.

patriotism   A person's love of his or her country.

pollution   Damage to the natural environment caused by human activities.

refugee   Someone who is forced to leave their home or country due to war, or because they are persecuted by their government or neighbours.

regime   A government. It may mean any kind of government, but is often used for a military government or dictatorship.

republic   A state that has no monarch. A republic is usually a democracy, with a president and a parliament elected by the people.

revolution   A violent change, usually of government, in which ordinary people take part. The name is sometimes given to other kinds of rapid change (such as the Industrial Revolution in the 19th century).

socialism   A form of government in which all the wealth of a country belongs to the people, not private owners.

statesman   A politician or government official of great ability, especially one who has an influence on international affairs.

suffrage   The right to vote.

superpowers   The most powerful states in the world. From 1945 to 1989 they were the USA and the Soviet Union.

technology   All the tools, instruments and methods used in industry and other forms of work, which were developed through scientific knowledge.

Third World   A name sometimes given to the poorer countries of the world, in Africa, Asia and Latin America.

trade union   An organisation to protect the rights of workers.

treasury   A place where money and valuables are kept. The word is used now for the department of government that controls finance.

tsar   The title, meaning 'emperor', of the ruler of Russia before the 1917 Revolution.

tyrant   A ruler who holds supreme power, above the law. It has become a name for an evil dictator who holds power by force.

welfare state   A state in which the government provides aid for people in need, such as the old, ill, handicapped, retired or unemployed.

Index

Index

Index

Acknowledgements

Picture research by Caroline Wood

The publisher would like to thank the following for illustrations:

Chris Brown; p17b
Peter Bull; p11cl,
Tim Clarey; p15tl, p27br, p39cr, p42
Gino D'Achille; back cover, p11t, p15tr, p19t, p25t, p33b, p35b, p40-41
Steve Noon; p20t, p29t, p36b,
Olive Pearson; all maps
Martin Sanders; p31tr

The publisher would like to thank the following for permission to use photographs:

Front cover Rex Features, p8l AKG; p8-9 BAL, "Galerie Daniel Malingue,Paris,France"; p9cr Jean-Loup Charmet, "Musée National de L'Education, Rouen"; p10-11b ET, "The Imperial War Museum,London"; p12tr, p12-13b, p13tr David King Collection; p14tr Mary Evans Picture Library; p14-15b "Special Collections Division, University of Washington Libraries Photo by Lee. Negative No.20102"; p16tl Hulton Getty; p16bl Magnum, Abbas; p16-17t, p18t, p18-19b Hulton Getty; p20bl Corbis, Hulton-Deutsch Collection; p20-21b "The Imperial War Museum, London"; p21tr, p22-23t Hulton Getty; p23b Magnum, Peter Marlow; p24t UNICEF; p24-25b Magnum, Koudelka; p26b Magnum, Bruno Barbey; p27cl Associated Press; p27 tr Magnum, Bruno Barbey; p28b Magnum, Abbas; p29bl Magnum, Bruno Barbey; p30 Magnum, Bruce Davidson; p31b Magnum, Raghu Rai; p32b SPL, John Mead; p32-33t SPL, Ed Young; p34-35t Magnum, Ferdinando Scianna; p35r Magnum, Rene Burri; p36t Magnum, Jean Gaumy; p37tr SPL, NASA; p37bl SPL, Ed Young; p38b Magnum, Gilles Peress; p38-39t Corbis, "Paul Velasco,ABPL".

Key: BAL = Bridgeman Art Library; BM = The British Museum; V&A = Victoria & Albert Museum; ET = E.T. Archive; SPL = Science Photo Library;
     AKG = AKG London; MH = Michael Holford

Sport and Fitness

UNCOVERED

*Other titles in the Careers Uncovered series
published by Trotman*

Accountancy Uncovered
E-Commerce Uncovered
Journalism Uncovered
Law Uncovered
Marketing & PR Uncovered
Media Uncovered
Medicine Uncovered
Music Industry Uncovered
Nursing & Midwifery Uncovered
Performing Arts Uncovered